SOUL SPARKS AND SPIRIT WHISPERS:

ON HEALING FROM TRAUMA & GRIEF

Katie Miller

DEDICATION & ACKNOWLEDGEMENTS

To the man who raised me as his own daughter, Gerald Francis Miller (1936-2024). He, along with my grandmother, Mary Patricia Miller, showed me unconditional love in the healthiest way I've ever known and for that I am eternally grateful. He was always there whenever I needed him, it didn't matter if it was the middle of the night. He taught me the value of working hard while knowing when to advocate for yourself in the workplace. He dedicated his life to his faith and his family, while still finding time to master his hobbies and interests. A humble man, he did not discriminate when it came to helping those in need, whether he knew them or not. These are lessons and values that I will carry with me always.

Secondly, I'd like to thank Napoleon Bonaparte Miller (2006-2019), for being the best friend in dog form that a little girl could ask for. My first brush with grief, he helped me transform that grief into pain. Some poems were originally written about the loss of my Napoleon, though since modified.

I'd like to acknowledge the people who have come into (and sometimes out of) my life to teach me the lessons I needed to learn, both painful and positive. It is also important to note those who have stayed, to give me advice on my life's journey and nudge me in the right direction. Because of these influences, I was given the strength to keep going and not give in to the darkness within, slowly forming a new outlook on life.

Table of Contents

ON GRIEF 4

22: ODE TO NAPOLEON 5

CLOUDY EYES 6

APRIL 20TH, 2024… 7

LETTER TO MY FATHERS 8

EXISTENTIAL DEPRESSION 9

WEED: PART 1 10

BROKEN HEART 11

PIANO SONG 12

WEED:PART2 13

WHAT'S LEFT BEHIND 14

TO THE ONES WHO WERE THERE 15

DARK NIGHT OF THE SOUL 16

GIFTED CHILD 17

MELANCHOLY SADNESS 18

THE BODY 19

FISHING 20

(GRAND) DAD 21

WISDOM/METAPHORS 22

REMEMBERANCE 23

GRANDPA 24

FALSE LOVE 27

TRUE LOVE 28

THE EDGE 29

CHILDHOOD INNOCENCE 31

ENERGY 32

HOPE 33

LIGHT 34

SEASONS 35

BIRDS KNOW 36

STARS 37

THE SNOWGLOBE 38

GENERATIONAL TRAUMA 39

ANCESTRAL HEALING 40

THE UNIVERSAL LAW 41

LETTER 42

THE QUIET WHISPER 43

LIFE'S BATTLEFIELD 44

SURVIVORS 45

RALLYING CRY 46

REBIRTH, RENEWAL, CHANGE 47

MOTHER EARTH 48

ON GRIEF

Why did you have to leave

Don't you know I scream,

Into the void that is my pillow

Every night, wishing you would come back

Or realize it was all a dream

Feeling like the end of everything

22: ODE TO NAPOLEON

The years fly by
Waiting to graduate high school
Blink and I'm 22
Lost without you

CLOUDY EYES

Watching you as you change,
Your eyes turn cloudy, and you stumble
While the world around you crumbles

Before it was you who took care of me
Teaching me how to walk and talk

It doesn't seem natural
As I grew up, you shrank down

Everything feels wrong now,
When will I feel strong enough,
To fix us

Somethings look so hopeless,
When your parents look so small

I wish you didn't have to go
Hole you left
Unimaginable

LETTER TO MY FATHERS

Saying goodbye to a dear friend,
Eyes open, not seeing
Disbelieving

Nothing to feel, this can't be real

Caught between a daze and that look on your face

Who will dry my tears,
When you are not there

Last looks, feeling shook
Must be brave
That look on your face

Auto pilot,
Snap out of it
Softly, I touch my hand to yours
Not yet cold, not still warm

Lingering for a beat, before leaving you behind

EXISTENTIAL DEPRESSION

Everything changed when you went away
It feels so hard for me to stay
When you're gone, how do I move on
People are partying, while I'm isolating

Getting high in my room,
Nothing to do without you

WEED: PART 1

10 years ago, I never thought this would be me
You're supposed to be the one smoking,
Tweaked out, toking

For the first time, I can finally see
Who I am is not who I want to be

Aiming to find the real me

BROKEN HEART

Crushing weight in my chest
Everything feels tense
Spots in front of my eyes
Can't hide from the darkness inside

PIANO SONG

I miss you right now, and I'll miss you tomorrow
Can time heal the sorrow

You've gone to the clouds
So I'll sit here and pray
Waiting for the day
When you come back down

WEED:PART2

How I used to love thee,
Instead, you have struck me

In your snare, I am entrapped
Willpower, I do lack
You are the gift I must send back

WHAT'S LEFT BEHIND

Reduced to a pile of jeans
Caught somewhere in between
Everything feels like a dream

I hate that you had to leave,
For me to figure out everything

WEED (again)

Why can't I be happy

Without copious amounts of weed

There are people that need me,

Things have never looked this good

Instead of embracing the day,

I get lost in the feeling of flying,

Weightless, among the clouds

It sucks to come down

Tired and bland,

Who smashed my head in?

Disillusionment

TO THE ONES WHO WERE THERE

He wasn't there

For baseball games and school plays,

Missed weekends,

Nights you could have spent with your friends

He wasn't there,

Look to the people who care

DARK NIGHT OF THE SOUL

Is this all there is?

Thinking back to when I was a kid

I wanted to make something of myself

Instead I'm left with all consuming doubt

The plays and talent shows,

Cast aside for smoking dope

Trapped inside my mind

Making up alibis `

For why I should hide

GIFTED CHILD

Gifted child, why don't you smile
Remember when you ran the miracle mile

Experiencing symptoms of the affliction
That is the social disease

Experiencing everything, try not to be so negative please
They lash out at what they cannot perceive

MELANCHOLY SADNESS

Never going to smile, no one left
To walk me down the aisle

They say time heals all wounds,
I still think of you
Eternally grateful
Your suffering removed

Safe in their arms, you're home

THE BODY

Though the body is gone
I know pieces of the soul live on
Scattered in the souls of those we've touched

FISHING

In the cool breeze,

I can see what you mean to me

We cast our lines,

I get a bite

When I think of the fish on the hook,

I start to cry

We throw it back into the brook

I cast my line

(GRAND) DAD

Making up for your son,
You provided unconditional love
Paid for my surgery,
Setting boundaries

Nobody was perfect but you were
Perfect to me
One day we'll go bowling
Until then, I'll sit here
wistfully

WISDOM/METAPHORS

The lamp illuminates when rewired with care
Almost nothing is broken beyond repair
Patience and wisdom are what he left
His wife was his best friend

REMEMBERANCE

Math homework, doctor's appointments, lightbulb assignments,
Lost in a book, walking down the hall after school
Gently chastised
Worry and love, my unofficial chauffeur

Help anyone out,
Didn't even know her
With hard work and love,
A great electrician

GRANDPA

They say not all heroes wear capes
All you need is to have what it takes
To do the right thing

If you called him, day or night
He would make it right
To bail you out of jail
Or grab you off the streets
Take you where you need to be

He won't take your money
He just wants to see you happy

He taught me determination and love
Get the job done
And always join the union

FALSE LOVE

It starts young, that gnawing in the gut

The longing to be loved

If you were never loved,

How can you love?

As you age, the hurt stays

Festering like a wound that cannot heal

The one thing that cannot be begged, borrowed, or stealed

Love cannot be found underground,

In seedy bars and teenaged basements

Cannot be snorted, injected, settling for less

With no place to call home,

Everyone ends up cold and alone

Can't love someone else

If you've never learned to love yourself

For that, you must unlock the true meaning of unconditional love

TRUE LOVE

Love is unconditional,
There for you at your worst, happy for your best
It nurtures you, guiding you to find your way

Love is annoying, misunderstood
The slamming of doors and shouting ensues
Not afraid of the blues,
It teaches you the power of forgiveness

Love is the strength to fight another day,
Nothing more, nothing less

THE EDGE

You found me standing on the precipice

When I was tired of it all

But you wouldn't let me fall

Here's to 29

Feeling so Divine

Previously lost

In Space & Time

Finally realigned to my purpose

We've got this

CHILDHOOD INNOCENCE

Banging pots and pans,
Remembering who I am
I am woman, I am man
I am part of the divine plan

ENERGY

Manifesting
No longer convalescing
Doing things for me
May not always get what I want But I
always get what I need

We are free
To be happy

Letting go of hangups
No longer caring what
others think of me
Going to think positively

Manifest destiny
Abundance and good loving
Going to be who I want to be
Young, wild and free

HOPE

You were the one who gave me hope,
When all I wanted was to be alone

Comforting me in my darkest hour,
With renewed strength, I begin to rise
Like a flower

LIGHT

You are the light

Trying to take flight

Only you can decide,

What you want to do with your life

When you listen to your heart

You will know what's right

SEASONS

The birds are chirping, singing their song

Reminding me that life goes on

Winter's biting chill gives way to Spring's drizzling rain

Summer comes again

Sweltering heat doesn't last that long, school starts in the Fall

Autumn leaves die as Winter comes again

Rebirth, Renewal, Change

Things can't stay the same

BIRDS KNOW

A breeze in the air,
Birds chirping without a care

Chirping and flapping,
Chittering and chattering

What do they see,
So high up in those trees

STARS

Sleeping under the stars
Each twinkling star a sign
That I am meant to be alive

Smell the dewy grass,
See the doe laying in the grass
While the ducks slowly pass

The true meaning of life

THE SNOWGLOBE

Our lives are like snow globes

When we are not aligned

Shiva the Divine (Destroyer)

Shakes it up

To resist means not living in alignment

with our highest good

To accept means achieving
Everything in your wildest dreams

There is but one precaution
One must learn to lead a life of discernment

GENERATIONAL TRAUMA

Generational Trauma
Starts with your mama
They want you to lay down
We won't back down

Gnashing our teeth, setting our jaws
We will right these wrongs

ANCESTRAL HEALING

Wars will rage

As they fight to turn the page

Through fire, there is cleansing rain

THE UNIVERSAL LAW

Through all the trauma and abuse
Lies a Truth Universal to you
The Law of One will protect you
When put to good vibrational use

LETTER

To my brothers and sisters,
Strength comes from quiet whispers

Strong, empowered women & men
Set sail
Justice will prevail

THE QUIET WHISPER

Strength like a quiet whisper

Moves boulders

Shouldering them like pebbles

LIFE'S BATTLEFIELD

We are the divine, having a human experience

Take what resonates, leave the rest

We will win this war

When we reveal our scars

Don't try so hard

Live authentically

You are the warrior,

This is your story

SURVIVORS

I survived, proving that I can stay alive
And thrive

I am empowered by their stories
That ones that I read, before me
Who proved that "Not bad enough" *is* bad enough

Don't let them tell you otherwise, with their fake smiles and alibis
We will continue to rise
And stay true to ourselves
Because we went through hell,
And live to tell the tale

RALLYING CRY

I won't back down from this fight,

I will stand up for what's right

I will yell

So loud they won't be able to drown out my screams

Screw the patriarchy

The dreamers, schemers, & heart bleeders

This is my call

Together we will rise, rise above it all

United we stand, divided we fall

As long as my heart beats from my breast,

I refuse to be oppressed

REBIRTH, RENEWAL, CHANGE

Like a Phoenix rises from the ashes I am striking the matches
On everything that no longer serves

Me and divinity

Burning flames,
There is a better way
-Rebirth, renewal, change-

MOTHER EARTH

Let the energy flow through the roots of Mother Earth

Pulsing through the souls of everyone

Let our hearts beat as one with the sound of a drum

And open our pineal glands to the frequency of love

Earth Mother,

Sky Father,

We beseech you

Please help your sons and daughters